OCPD BONDAGE
and Spiritual Warfare!

The *Hidden* Knowledge

– to the **Puzzle** of Insight –

– Is Now REVEALED!

A Startling Revelation of the <u>Direct</u> Connection *between* OCPD and Demonic Influence

OCPD BONDAGE
and Spiritual Warfare!

Relationships! – *Can be* <u>*Transformed!*</u>

– *Tormented* Minds – <u>FREED!</u>

Acquire this Knowledge! *–For* YOU Who Are the OCPD Person, *or* for <u>YOUR</u> OCPD Loved One – <u>Without Delay!</u>

Published by **New Frontier Health Research**

Cover design by Mack W. Ethridge

Library of Congress Cataloging-in-Publications
Data, Ethridge, Mack W.

OCPD Bondage and Spiritual Warfare! –
Complete edition

1st Complete Softback Edition
April 2015

ACKNOWLEDGMENTS

I wish to humbly and reverently acknowledge the direct Guidance and Inspiration of the Holy Spirit, of whom Jesus is the personification in Heaven and on earth. I thank them both, profoundly, for their providing me with the highly interpersonal experiences necessary to come to understand OCPD in great *depth* and sophistication (though the coming by this Knowledge was immensely painful) and for equipping me with the absolutely necessary observational, analytical, and writing abilities so crucial to the conveying of vital knowledge on this subject to those individuals so greatly in need of it. And, of course, I heartfeltly thank God the Father, the Supreme Creator and God of Love, Whom, I believe, commissioned me to research and write this volume that untold numbers of OCPD people, worldwide, and those who love them and interact with them, *may find their way to deliverance* from all the heartache and hardship OCPD imposes upon them, men and women, mostly all of goodwill, actually, everywhere. And, lastly, I thank you, Lord, that this '**Search** [for *Insight*] **and Rescue** [of tormented OCPD souls] **Operation**', in manual form, has been launched upon the Sea of Humanity – with, I pray, your full Blessing!

Dedication

This Research Report, and Life Instruction Manual, is dedicated to the *hundreds of thousands* of people worldwide, who, *up till now*, have had to live with the devastating effects of **Obsessive-Compulsive Personality Disorder** (OCPD) upon their lives, and upon the lives of those they love, with <u>little</u> to <u>no</u> hope for **total** and **complete deliverance**. That dismal prospect, with the publication of this book, has **now** come to a most welcome end! Should you be one such person, I want you to know that **full deliverance** is possible, particularly when there is willing cooperation between you, the OCPD person and God (but, also, even between the *Non*-OCPD person and God, as you will learn!), and the scientifically, and *Scripturally-informed,* recommendations based on unchanging Spiritual Principals or Law. To your **commitment** to finding your deliverance in its fullness, I **applaud** you! And I **highly esteem** you for reaching for **all** that our Creator so earnestly desires you obtain! And may 'your time' to be **set free** be NOW, with no further senseless delays by OCPD, self-imposed barriers, which you can **now**, by the application of new knowledge, and *with God's Grace*, begin to dismantle – **one-by-one**!

Disclaimer

All recommendations in this book are not in any fashion to be construed as medical or psychiatric advice, either for physical, mental, emotional, or psychological ailments, or for spiritual afflictions. This research paper is not intended to diagnose the existence of OCPD, nor to prescribe treatment. In short, this book is meant for informational purposes, only. Before putting into practice any of its ideas or concepts, you would be well-advised to consult a certified health professional and/or a trusted spiritual advisor or counselor, conversant with these matters. Further, while these principles have proven effective for many individuals, the degree of success any <u>particular</u> OCPD person or *non*-OCPD person may attain in utilizing the suggested recommendations is dependent upon a multitude of factors, including, but not limited to, the OCPD person's or *non*-OCPD person's level of intelligence, psychological state, personal temperament, physical condition, determination to succeed, skillfulness in application of the life principles, and perhaps, most important of all, the *character* and *quality* of this person's personal relationship with God. The author expressly disavows any responsibility for the reader's use or misuse of any part of this work, including all spiritual disciplines and practices, though they are widely recognized by various authorities as safe, beneficial, and worthwhile endeavors.

Beloved

[*Dear* Heart

Who has OCPD],

I *Wish*

Above <u>All</u> Things,

That Thou

Mayest **Prosper**

And

<u>Be</u> in [*Complete*

Mental] **Health**

III John 1:2

(Adapted)

Author Qualifications

Mack Ethridge is uniquely qualified as no other person alive today to author *'When OCPD Meets the Power of God!'* as he is America's premier OCPD lay expert, having written the world's first and *only* comprehensive textbook and original, innovative workbooks on Obsessive Compulsive Personality Disorder, supplying his best-selling treatment and recovery volumes to the North Shore/Long Island Health Care System in New York; and he is also a leading expert on little-known, also new and restored, specialized aspects of Biblical knowledge (concerning our astounding Identity in Christ, claiming our Freedom in Christ, exercising our Authority in Christ, and, perhaps most importantly, obtaining the Deliverance available through Christ, at every level of our beings, including mental/emotional/psychological, as well as spiritual); whose books are in the private libraries of such world notables as Professor N.T. Wright, Andy Andrews, Claire Pfann, Marilla Ness, Akiane Kramarik, Tony Robbins, and Pastor Joel Osteen. And he heads the Mercy Rose Ministries Worldwide Outreach, in operation, now, for nine years, as its Founder and Operational Director. And with profound, scholarly Insights into the psychological makeup and inner motivations of OCPD people, arrived at through *thousands of hours*, spanning a number of years, of research, ongoing direct, intimate contact, interaction with, and keen observation of OCPD persons, and Mack's intensive decades-long heart search into the spiritual depths of authentic Biblical Christianity, Mack stands wholly unequalled among OCPD researchers, writers, and instructors, as well as clearly unmatched among Christian ministers, teachers, and counselors, in his ability to convey Vital, life-freeing practices, disciplines, and Truths to OCPD people in the capacity of Master Teacher and Christian Scholar/Counselor, par excellence! This one-of-a-kind psycho-spiritual combination of knowledge, skills, and heavenly communication gift of Mack's, so expertly synthesized, has produced a volume destined to become a trailblazing classic in the annals of OCPD Hope for Healing messages and Practices, and Illuminated Philosophy, for the OCPD person to safeguard and preserve their new-found, or rather newly-*bestowed* Freedom and Deliverance, and Victory, from Above – *at long last!*

Personal Letter to Reader

Dear friend,

We here at Mercy Rose Ministries are overjoyed that you have found your way to this vital Life-Liberating Message needed to be heard by so many suffering OCPD people, and those who interact with them on a recurring basis, today. This special, extended brochure-book contains the *essential* findings of the author originally presented in his ground-breaking (source) volume, **When OCPD Meets the Power of God**, regarding the certain connection between OCPD and the 'fallen realm' of angels.

Every textual presentation, every tabular presentation, every listing, every carefully-composed prayer, every historical reference, every geographical reference, every special 'pocket card' designed for the expulsion of demons, every reference to the official position of scientists regarding this matter, and *considerably more*, are **all** incorporated herein under one cover as a single, unified theme for ready referral, mental grasp, and application to your life.

No attempt has been made to intersperse even transitional paragraphs between the various sections (which have appeared in *various* parts of the source volume, **When OCPD Meets the Power of God**), as the themes speak for themselves, and have no need for such, due to the natural, logical flow of complementary ideas one section to another.

It is, therefore, the heartfelt wish of the entire Mercy Rose Ministries staff that you will derive maximal benefit from this trail-blazing work, and be inspired to acquire the 'mother' work, as well, to the end that you may have the total OCPD picture relative to **ALL** the causes for lack of 'Insight' in the OCPD person, and what the remedies for those challenges have been found to be.

Sincere well-wishes for freedom from all invisible, yet wholly real, negative influences from any realm, source, or being! **God bless you!**

Table of Contents

Ephesians 6:12

'For we wrestle not against flesh and blood, but against **Principalities**, against **Powers**, against the **Rulers of the darkness of this world**, against **spiritual wickedness** in high places.'

Saint Paul

Make no mistake about it, OCPD, in its *full-blown* state, is nothing less than devastating. It rips asunder marriages, causing ongoing peace-destroying strife, often resulting in the two married (or domestic) partners being unable to live with each other. Separations occur, and divorces follow. Reconciliations are impossible. The children of such stricken marriages, or relationships, suffer terribly, and sustain irreparable damage as they see their beloved parents, instead of caring for and loving each other, arguing and battling with each other interminably. And perhaps worse, still, is the case where the OCPD parent unleashes their dysfunction toward the children *day in* and *day out*. Children who have no defense against their sick parent's harsh words and threatening behaviors. Children who will bear the scars of their ill parent's mistreatment for as long as they live. Non-spousal relationships are certainly not spared the trauma of OCPD assaults, either, where the brother of an OCPD sister feels the full brunt of their harassment, and insanity; or a daughter (or son) is singled out by an OCPD parent to receive the brunt of their tormenting attention. The sense of there being 'a black cloud' hovering over or permeating the home is not uncommon, bringing a sense of foreboding – and even *doom*. Doom that the relationship will most surely, *eventually*, totally collapse, becoming unbearable to the non-OCPD person, and that the former security and stability of home life will be a thing of the past. Then, all the attendant fears of where will the non-OCPD person go, or stay, etc., will haunt their mind, *particularly* if this 'victim' of another's OCPD is not in the best financial condition in their own right, and perhaps may not even have a steady, sufficient, and/or reliable source of income, or even a job at that point. A further complication can be that the normal person may have health problems which only add to the apprehension of what their leaving the OCPD person, to preserve their own sanity, might mean for them. Will that prohibit them from obtaining gainful employ-ment, or their qualifying for obtaining a lease. Frightening prospects, all.

OCPD is a condition wherein some of the most destructive and undesirable *intra*-personal and *inter*-personal relationship traits find expression in one unfortunate individual.

Much of what God never intended for people to experience and exhibit are prominently manifested through these traits. For these traits by their very nature are <u>*counter-productive*</u>, <u>*uncooperative*</u>, <u>*domineering*</u>, <u>*abrasive*</u>, <u>*abusive*</u>, <u>*distasteful*</u>, <u>*harmful*</u>, <u>*disruptive*</u>, <u>*devastating*</u>, <u>*damaging*</u>, <u>*enslaving*</u>, <u>*punishing*</u>, and to be completely blunt, <u>*insane*</u>! They are *the traits of the world, which lives apart from God,* **magnified** to a tremendous degree! – To which even Christians are <u>*not*</u> immune.

Only those who are intimately associated with these people can understand the ***far-reaching*** destructive consequences of the OCPD person's speech and actions, and the human casualties that are incurred and that lay scattered all about them. OCPD is an unrelenting assault on Life Itself! A dark cover! A suffocating atmosphere! Really, a 'curse'!

In biblical terms, the OCPD person embodies and exercises many pronounced traits of the <u>*fallen*</u> flesh and its carnality: selfishness, inconsiderateness, pride, arrogance, stubbornness, grudge-bearing (unforgiving), condemning (judging), fault-finding (criticizing), and much, <u>*much*</u> more.

Right here, however, I hasten to add that <u>*in no way*</u> should the above description be interpreted as a **judgment** or a **condemnation** on the OCPD person, labelling them as 'bad' or 'evil' – <u>*neither*</u> of which they are. As they are as much a 'victim' of their own mental illness, as are those around them. It is just a truthful recitation of their many ingrained characteristics that so <u>*interfere*</u> with **healthful**, **beneficial**, and **enjoyable** living practices, which when taken together make life, as God intended, so wholly worthwhile!

(See next page listing for a <u>clear</u> <u>contrast</u> between two opposing states.)

An assault on Life	*vs.*	A cultivation of Life
A repudiation of Truth	*vs.*	A declaration of Truth
A compliance with darkness	*vs.*	An alliance with Light
A denial of others' rights	*vs.*	A validation of others' rights
A major step toward insanity	*vs.*	A leisurely stroll into sanity
An abandonment of Faith	*vs.*	An embracing of Faith
A discarding of Hope	*vs.*	A celebration of Hope
A forfeiture of Love	*vs.*	A joining with Love
An unhealthy exalting of self	*vs.*	A healthy debasing of self
A bearer of ill-will	*vs.*	An exemplar of Good-will
A perfectionistic nightmare	*vs.*	A pursuer of Excellence
A relationship strainer	*vs.*	A relationship nurturer
A straight jacket on creativity	*vs.*	A flowering of innovative ideas
A decreer of doom	*vs.*	A prognosticator of blessing
A master creator of hardship	*vs.*	An attitude of ease of expression

NOTE: Clearly, the contradistinction between these two states of being (one unnatural and *abnormal*, the other natural and *normal*) are dramatic, and profoundly highlight why OCPD **must** be addressed and overcome.

Christ's Heart Prayer
(Adapted)

Father, the Hour Is Come
Glorify *Thy* Son,

That *Thy* Son Also May **Glorify** Thee.
As Thou Hast Given Him **Power** Over _ALL_ flesh,
That He Should **Give Eternal Life** [*free* from **all**
obsessions and compulsions] to as Many as Thou
Hast Given Him.
And This *IS* **Life Eternal**, That they [**all** former
OCPD sufferers, *now* delivered!] Might Know **Thee**,
The _Only_ True God, And *Jesus Christ*,
Whom **Thou** – Hast Sent!
(John 17:1-3)

May the **Blessing** of the Saviour – be Upon You!

Remember,

God is the **Source**

of ***All*** Insight,

No Matter the Avenue,

Or

Channel of Expression,

through Which

It Comes.

Therefore, Look to Him

First,

And **be more surely sped along**

– to *your* Healing

And

Deliverance!

There are seven identifiable arenas of damage or dysfunction in (or related to) the being of man where the absence of Insight may originate, each arena suggesting its <u>own</u> respective possible cause of malfunction in OCPD people.

The **first** arena to be suspect is the corporeal (physical) brain. The brain may be malformed, or it may have been damaged somehow from, or since, birth. There may be a congenital deformity, proceeding from a genetic defect. Or, there may even be a metabolic, or electro-chemical dysfunction in operation. Modern medical diagnostic machines, such as a magnetic resonance imaging (MRI) device, can often uncover whether or not the brain is abnormal in some way. Although, there is <u>no</u> <u>one</u> <u>specific</u> structural abnormality detected to date thought to be the **sole** culprit of OCPD symptoms, some major correlations to diseased brain tissue, or injuries, have been found. (Discussed more at length, later)

The **second** arena to be suspect is the incorporeal (<u>non</u>-physical) mind. The invisible 'mental body', and/or its theorized component parts, may be defective somehow from birth, though manifestation of dysfunction may not become evident till the adolescent years. Thankfully, psycho-therapy (particularly, various forms of Cognitive-Behavioral Therapy) has been shown effective to the degree the OCPD person has, or acquires Insight; but, more importantly, proceeds to translate such Insight into action.

The **third** arena to be suspect is the actual organ of the physical heart, which may well be the repository of an <u>inter</u>-dimensional soul, or spirit. This wonder of *much more* than a pump is now known to not only <u>feel</u> though emotion experienced, but also to 'think' through it *cerebral-type cells* and communicate directly with the physical brain cells. This is a whole new field of research which is little explored relative to OCPD dysfunctional traits, to date.

The **fourth** arena to be suspect is what the Scriptures call 'the flesh', or the lower, _fallen_ _nature_ of man; also called 'the old man'. The designation of 'flesh' is used here in the Biblical sense of man's 'sin proneness' and proclivity to violate the laws of Love. Unfortunately, in the OCPD person, this predisposition to transgress the laws of respectful human conduct are often _greatly_ pronounced, or _highly_ exaggerated relative to many of the OCPD traits. Yet, Scripture offers several antidotes, as you will see.

The **fifth** arena to be suspect is what is called 'faulty socialization', particularly, in one's family of origin. Faulty parental rearing practices have been implicated, though not definitively proven. Although, the home environment, no doubt, plays a role, here, in some instances. No universally accepted answers or solutions have been found to _head off_ these early life occurrences. Yet, psycho-therapy can be helpful, again, provided Insight arises, and corrective action is taken.

The **sixth** arena to be suspect involves (usually _unseen_) malevolent spiritual forces. Serious, and well-credentialed, _paranormal_ research scientists are bringing greater recognition to the field of parapsychology than ever before, establishing legitimacy and increasing respectability, as well. And, though skeptical Orthodox science, as a whole, still offers no help here, Scripture offers highly practical, effective, and explicit means to successfully deal with such entities.

And, the **seventh** arena to be suspect (though _many_ would not suspect so) is that of a Benevolent Power, meaning God, or his angelic emissaries. Strange as it may initially seem, the Creator may be the principal cause of a person's OCPD, actually meant for that person's _ultimate_ good! And without a doubt, should this be the case, that person's complete healing is already predetermined to occur by God's decree.

(See _corresponding_ _table_ on next page for a correlation of all the above)

The <u>Primary</u> Arenas where the *Absence* of Insight May Originate and Their *<u>Possible</u>* Causes in OCPD People

Arena of Damage or <u>Dysfunction</u>	<u>Cause</u>	<u>Remedy</u> (or *No*)
1		
Physical Brain	The brain may be mal-formed or damaged somehow *from birth* due to a genetic defect, a subsequent injury, or a metabolic (electro-chemical) dysfunction.	No <u>one</u> **specific** *structural* abnormality detected to date is thought to be capable of producing <u>all</u> OCPD Insight deficits. But intriguing hints exist. (See page 27)
2		
Non-physical Mind	The invisible 'mental body', and/or its theorized components, may be defective somehow *from birth*. Manifestation may not be evident, however, till adolescence.	Psycho-therapy has been shown effective *to the degree* the OCPD person has, or acquires, 'Insight', and translates that insight into **action**.
3		
Physical Heart (and its inner *inter*-dimensional soul, or spirit)	The physical heart is now known to not only *feel* (through emotion) but 'think' (through *its* cerebral-*type* cells.) It may be there's some deficiency present in either. [1]	This is a whole new area of research as yet *little* explored relative to OCPD. Helpful answers are likely to be forthcoming. (For some **amazing** facts, see page 29)

4 Flesh (lower, fallen nature, also called 'the old man')	The term 'flesh', here, is used in the biblical sense of one's *'sin proneness'* or one's natural attraction/desire to violate a moral, ethical, or spiritual law.	In the OCPD person, this predisposition to transgress the laws of love and respectful human interaction are highly *exaggerated* relative to many traits. Yet, Scripture, offers *specific* antidotes here.
5		
Faulty *socialization* in family of origin	Faulty parental upbringing has been implicated, though not proven. The home environment, no doubt, plays a role, in some instances.	No known universally applicable answers or solutions have been found here. Psychotherapy can be helpful, again, provided 'Insight' arises, and correspondingly appropriate **action** is taken.
6		
Malevolent Forces (See page 162)	Serious *paranormal research scientists* are bringing legitimacy to a formerly ridiculed or ignored field.	Orthodox science offers no help, here, yet, Scripture offers **explicit** means and methods of remedy.
7		
Benevolent Power (See page 32)	Strange as it may *initially* seem, **God** may be the primary cause of another's OCPD, meant for the person's ultimate good.	Without a doubt, should this be the case, a time of gradual (or sudden) healing is predetermined to occur at God's decree.

[1] The Institute of **HeartMath**, Boulder Creek, CA, is an internationally recognized nonprofit research and education organization.

Scriptures Implicating Satan to Be the Source of *Lack* of Insight in Certain Groups of People and Individuals

(As the *Chief fallen angel* who attempts to *thwart* God's Purpose in our Lives)

Scripture Citation	Bible Verse	Commentary
Matt. 13:18, 19	Hear ye therefore the parable of the sower. When anyone heareth the word of the kingdom, and understands it *not*, then cometh the wicked one, and *catches away* that [seed of Truth] which was sown in his heart.	Jesus is informing us, in the clearest of language, that knowledge (**Insight**) planted in a person's heart by God can be 'caught away' by Satan, or prevented from *taking root*, leaving unawareness, only.
II Cor. 4:3, 4	But if our gospel be **hid**, it is **hid** to them that are lost [to themselves]: in whom the **god** of *this* [fallen] **world** hath **blinded** the minds of them which believe *not*, lest **the Light** of the glorious gospel of Christ, Who is the image of God, should shine unto them.	When someone is *oblivious* to something (as is *often* the case with OCPD people), they have no knowledge of it; it is, in effect, 'hid' from them. And Satan hides much Truth from OCPD people by blinding their inner *mental 'eyes'* to comprehend and 'see'.
I John 4:6, second half	Hereby know we the [Holy] Spirit of Truth, and the [profane, evil] **spirit** of error.	Much of what the OCPD person *falsely* believes to be true originates from this spirit of error.

Scripture Citation	Bible Verse	Commentary
Eph. 4:17, 18	Henceforth walk not as other Gentiles walk, in the vanity of their mind, having [their] understanding darkened, [Insight *diminished*] being alienated from the life of God through the ignorance [*lack* of Insight] that is in them, because of the blindness of their heart [to that which was sown *by God* in their heart].	It would seem [that God] who *delivers* us from the power of darkness (the influence of Satan and his demonic underlings) (Col. 1:13), often does so through our 'increasing in the knowledge of God' (Col. 1:10). For it is the Insight acquired that will 'heal' the blindness, and *restore* mental sight to OCPD.
Roman 8:5	For ye have not received the [evil] spirit of bondage again to fear; but ye have received the [Holy]spirit of adoption, whereby we cry, Abba, Father.	The spirit of bondage is both the person of Satan, *and* is the 'wavelength' he broadcasts to cloud, or darken, human minds, including OCPD people.
II Cor. 10:4	For the weapons of our warfare are *not* carnal, but mighty through God to the pulling down of [mental, demonic] strongholds; casting down imaginations [*false* thought].	The phenomenon of the *absence* of Insight, in otherwise intelligent people, can *no* doubt, often be attributed to evil spirits. But, best rule out other possibilities first.

NOTE: Lack of Insight *can* be a **powerful** demonic stronghold over an individual.

Truth

I, Truth, am thy Redeemer, come to Me   *(Isaiah 48:17)*;

Lay down thy sin and pain and wild unrest;

And I will calm thy spirit's stormy sea   *(Mark 4:39)*,

Pouring the oil of peace upon thy breast:

Friendless and lone – lo, **I abide with thee**   *(Hebrews 13:5)*.

Defeated and deserted, cast away,

What refuge hast thou? Whither canst thou fly?

Upon my changeless breast thy burdens lay;

I am thy certain refuge, even I   *(Psalm 91:2)*:

All things are passing; I alone can stay.

Lo **I**, the Great Forsaken, **am the Friend**

Of the forsaken; I, whom men despise   *(Isaiah 53:3)*,

The weak, the helpless, and despised defend;

I gladden aching hearts and weeping eyes;

Rest thou in Me, **I am thy sorrow's end**   *(Rev. 21:4)*.

Lovers and friends and wealth, pleasures and fame –

These fail and change, and pass into decay;

But **My Love does not change**   *(Jeremiah 31:3)*; and in thy blame

I blame thee not, nor turn my face away *(John 8:15)*:

In My calm bosom hide thy sin and shame.   – Anonymous
(John 14:6, I AM **The Truth**, Jesus the Christ!)

This Truth Pronouncement (Soliloquy) is *especially* relevant to OCPD

Christ's Perfect Exchange

(Adapted)

I AM the **Living Bread** which *Came Down* from Heaven [sent to **ALL** OCPD sufferers]:

If *Any* Man Eat of **This** Bread, **He** Shall Live *Forever* [and even **NOW**, be *freed* from **all** OCPD tendencies]: And the Bread that I Will Give Is **My Flesh**, Which I Will Give for the **Life of the World** [and for *your* return to mental health]. And, **All** that the Father Giveth Me *Shall Come* to Me; and **Him** that Cometh to Me, I Will in *No Wise* Cast Out.

(John 6:51, 37)

May the **Assurance** of the Saviour – **Establish** Your Heart Today!

PRAYER for an OCPD Loved One

(Example)

Dear Heavenly Father, Lord, I come before you, today, in heartfelt thanksgiving for the privilege and opportunity to do so. I **know** that you are **the Living God** who hears *every* prayer that I pray, and that my prayers are *always* answered by you! I praise you, this day, Lord, for the gift of Life, and for all the many blessings that are mine. You are my unfailing Source, **my Light** and **my Salvation**, and will be all the days of my life.

Father, I come to you, now, in the precious and incomparable Name of my Lord and Saviour, Jesus Christ of Nazareth, through Whom I can have *total* **Confidence**, and **Certainty**, that I <u>WILL</u> be granted the petitions I make of you. And, Lord, I just want to thank you, in <u>advance</u>, for your ANSWERING my prayer for the healing and deliverance of my loved one, _____ , who is greatly burdened with OCPD.

I respectfully, yet <u>boldly</u>, ask that *every* obsession, *every* compulsion, and *every* erroneous belief that besets _____ be **banished** from his/her being, and that *no* relapse will ever occur! I ask that you, Lord, will grant this beloved child of yours whatever **INSIGHT** they require to be set free from their torturing affliction – to serve <u>YOU</u>.

And, Lord, should there be <u>hidden</u> and <u>unseen</u>, detrimental *'influences'* from <u>*ANY*</u> realm, source, or being tormenting my loved one, then through the *unassailable* **Authority** and *unconquerable* **Power** of my Lord and Saviour Jesus Christ, I DECLARE that your overshadowing protection envelop this loved one, and *drive* any such influences *away*! And **in <u>FULL</u> faith** I rest **assured** you are attending to this matter, and that at the appointed time, Lord, you <u>WILL</u> set my loved one free!

Nevertheless, ***<u>Thy</u>*** Will be done in all things, Lord, and thank you! *<u>Amen</u>!*

– for *him*

Heavenly Father, I thank you that you always hear the burdens on my heart. And I come to you, now, in behalf of my brother _____, whom I believe is *being **influenced** and **oppressed** by unclean spirits*. I'm convinced this is so, Lord, because I see such **pronounced** OCPD traits in my brother, which traits amount to *nothing less* than **mental** and **emotional addictions** which force him to perpetually indulge in hurtful obsessions and, unthinkingly, act out harmful compulsions. Therefore, I sense there is a greater, sinister, invisible power at work, here, which is, to all intents and purposes, **harassing** and **goading** him to think and perform in illogical, irrational, and nonsensical ways on a routine basis. Acting in good faith, then, Lord, and knowing you have **granted Authority** to believers over *all* unclean spirits, I boldly declare the following: Satan! And unclean spirits! **In the name of Jesus**, and by the **Unassailable Power of His shed blood**, and by the Authority *invested* in me, I COMMAND you to come out of him! You are **defeated foes**! And I adjure you to *NEVER* return to this brother, again! And it is so, Amen!

Christ Sanctioned Expulsion Ritual

– for **her**

Heavenly Father, I thank you that you always hear the burdens on my heart. And I come to you, now, in behalf of my sister _____, whom I believe is *being **influenced** and **oppressed** by unclean spirits*. I'm convinced this is so, Lord, because I see such **pronounced** OCPD traits in my sister, which traits amount to *nothing less* than **mental** and **emotional addictions** which force her to perpetually indulge in hurtful obsessions and, unthinkingly, act out harmful compulsions. Therefore, I sense there is a greater, sinister, invisible power at work, here, which is, to all intents and purposes, **harassing** and **goading** her to think and perform in illogical, irrational, and nonsensical ways on a routine basis. Acting in good faith, then, Lord, and knowing you have **granted Authority** to believers over *all* unclean spirits, I boldly declare the following: Satan! And unclean spirits! **In the name of Jesus**, and by the **Unassailable Power of His shed blood**, and by the Authority *invested* in me, I COMMAND you to come out of her! You are **defeated foes**! And I adjure you to *NEVER* return to this sister, again! And it is so, Amen!

Christ's Comfort Promise
(Adapted)

Let **Not** Your *Heart* Be Troubled [you who have OCPD]:

Ye **Believe** in God, **Believe** *Also* in **Me**.
I Will **Not** Leave You Comfortless: I **Will** Come to YOU [and ***remove*** your obsessions and compulsions].
Because I Live, *Ye* Shall Live Also.
At That Day Ye Shall **Know** That **I AM** in My Father, and Ye [Are] in Me,
And **I in You**.

(John 14:1, 18-20)

May the **Peace** of the Saviour – be *Within* You!

Today!

With every rising of the Sun

Think of your life as just begun.

The Past has _cancelled_ and buried deep

All Yesterdays. There let them sleep!

Concern yourself with but **Today**.

Grasp it, and teach it to obey . . .

Your Will and plan. Since time began

Today has been the friend of man!

You and **Today!** A **_Soul sublime!_**

And the great heritage of time.

With God Himself to bind the twain,

Go forth, brave heart! Attain! _Attain!_

_By_ Ella Wheeler Wilcox

The following Mini-Essays were designed to *directly* address from a purely Scriptural perspective the wholly legitimate concerns of OCPD people relative to their, and others', Salvation.

Each Mini-Essay pertains to one (or more) of those concerns, all of which fall within one (or more) of **The True Christian Doctrines** tabular presentation categories preceding this page.

There are sixty-two Mini-Essays, in all, but these are *only* a *representative sample* of the essays found within the Author's twelve-year-long, life work, a 702-page compendium entitled:

The Divine Plan Revealed!

– The Ultimate Revelation of Life's Purpose and God's Destiny for Man!

(A detailed book review **Press Release** on The Divine Plan Revealed can be found toward the close of *this* book you hold in your hands.)

of SPECIAL NOTE: You, as the reader of **When OCPD Meets the Power of God**, will find this publication a tremendous <u>encouragement</u> and <u>relief</u> to what you have been told (erroneously) about God in the past. It can go a long ways in *hastening* your **deliverance** should your sensitivity be great. This volume is available from Amazon.com online.

The
Spirit
Of
Victory!

**(*Claim* It! Right <u>Now</u>!
– <u>*Today!*</u>)**

The **Critical,**
Often *Most* Important, Insight
Many Need to Acquire
if
They Are *Ever* to Be Rid of OCPD

– *in **this** Lifetime!*

(The next section explains)

Our best scientists, researchers, and psychologists, alike, are all at a loss to explain what is often *the total absence of Insight* in OCPD stricken people. **How is it** that these people, often highly intelligent and observant in many other respects, are so 'blind' to their own self-sabotaging ways? *Why* can they not 'see' what they are doing to themselves, and their fellows? **How can it** possibly be that what is so obvious to virtually everyone else, *they are oblivious to?* It simply just does not make sense. This, at present, is a great mystery at which investigators and deep thinkers are obliged to just throw up their hands, and turn away from – in stunned disbelief and perplexity. They have no answer, as the whole situation appears completely inexplicable!

Something is clearly prohibiting OCPD people from realizing the Truth about their behavior. It is as if a concealing, partitioning wall of darkness stands between them and Reality. Or, put another way, it is as if the OCPD person is viewing everyday life, its Reality, with extremely faulty lenses, obscuring and distorting what is directly in front of their faces.

The following are all proposed causes, or contributing factors, of OCPD: Poor or inadequate socialization, brain dysfunction or abnormality, genetic predisposition, etc. And these can all be factors – to be sure.

Yet, we are dealing with something, a mechanism or **compelling influence**, if you will, that renders a person's thinking distorted, negative and pessimistic, incomplete or partial, detrimental to one's self at nearly all levels, and which mechanism is *incapable of detection* (by the unsuspecting person, at least). It is 'cloaked' under thoughts, feelings, and impressions, which are made to 'feel right' to the OCPD person, yet are **absolutely wrong** in the sense of their deleterious effect upon the OCPD person, and those who are made to suffer along with them. How is this to be explained? What is shutting off the OCPD person's sight so effectively, so thoroughly? How are thoughts which are not *wholly* sane, made to <u>appear</u> sane, and be accepted by the OCPD person as true? And how is it that when irrefutable evidence to the contrary is presented, even by respected and acknowledged authorities, to the OCPD person, that their entire approach to life is backward and self-defeating, they <u>*still*</u> cannot see the falsity of their unjustifiable mental positions and behavioral stance? Fortunately, brave and free-thinking researchers **now** know!

The explanation, introduced earlier in this report, may surprise you, be unbelievable to you, startle you, and at first frighten you, but it is an explanation which totally accounts for every distressing symptom the OCPD person exhibits (particularly when in <u>*full*</u> and <u>unbridled</u> manifestation), and which others have to reluctantly, and often with dread, contend with. And this explanation accounts accurately for the OCPD person's total inability to extricate themselves from their predicament.

So here is, now, the simple, yet, all-enlightening explanation:

**The True, Underlying, Perpetuating Cause of OCPD
And Its Symptom Magnification *Is***

The **tremendous likelihood** that the OCPD person is being influenced by *invisible, malevolent intelligences,* which were well known to the intelligentsia, and lay persons, of the ancient world[1]; and whose existence and nefarious purposes are plainly set forth in Holy Scripture, as <u>*unclean spirits*</u>, <u>*evil spirits*</u>, or **demons**.

And that is the plain, experientially, historically, and scientifically verifiable Truth! Which *proof* is available to all **progressive** and **free-thinking** researchers of **courage** and **integrity** – and a <u>***passion***</u> for the Truth.

Such entities were widely recognized in the ancient world by their learned scholars, doctors, and even scientists. These entities constitute another 'life form' antagonistic, even hostile, to humans, whose sole reason for being is to subjugate, torment, and enslave people who 'open the door' to their entrance, and 'invite' these entities into their person and affairs. They are bent upon destroying people, and the OCPD person is the way he or she is, because such spirits have **invaded** their person, usually by *directing* their thoughts (through establishing their **mental focus**) and influencing their behaviors through faulty beliefs and defective philosophical postures. These intelligences *encourage* moods of self-pity, pessimism, and negativity by *magnifying* such feelings (through adding their **negative energies** to the OCPD person's own). These malevolent entities then 'feed' upon the drama created, and they take pleasure in the suffering caused by their **spiritual assault** upon this OCPD person's physical being and *non*-physical psyche (consisting of mind, soul, and spirit).

The first order of business of these malevolent entities is to deprive the person of mental and psychological **Light (or Insight)**, which *if* it were present, would safeguard the person from entertaining, fostering, and clinging to obsessions and compulsions, thereby becoming OCPD.

The central Scripture which corroborates this assertion is II Corinthians 4:3, 4 as follows, with appropriate OCPD adaptation:

> But if our gospel [Truth] be **hid** [veiled to *OCPD* sight],
> it is **hid** to them that are lost:
> ('lost' to *themselves*, only, but NOT to God's redeeming hand!)
>
> In whom **the god of this world** hath **blinded** the minds of them which believe not, lest the **Light** [Insight] of the **Glorious Gospel of Christ**, who is the image of God [or, of **Life Truth**], should shine unto them.

Now, let me hasten to add that there is no cause for alarm, here, as Satan, and his underlings, are permitted by God, *only for a time*, to **obscure** (or, **blind**, an individual to) the Great Truths of Life, whether those Truths be *Gospel* Truths, or whether those Truths be *Life* **Truths** – in general. This 'blindness' is NOT a permanent condition relative to one's future Salvation, nor even to one's state of conscious awareness, or **Insight**, in this temporal life, necessarily. The blindness can, and will be, easily lifted by God in His wisdom at a time of His choosing.

The principle of *demonic-induced* blindness, resulting in ignorance, is further alluded to in the following Scriptures:

> When any one hears the word of the kingdom [or any word of Truth], and understands it not, **then cometh the wicked one [or his cohorts], and *catches away* [or removes the faculty of discernment] that which was sown in his heart [Gospel Truth, or *Life Truth*, by extension].** Matthew 13:19

> For ye have not received **the [demonic] spirit of bondage** again **to fear** [which underlies much OCPD behavior]; but ye have received the Spirit of adoption, whereby we cry, Abba, Father. Romans 8:15

> Be sober, be vigilant; because your adversary the devil, as a roaring lion, walks about, seeking whom he may 'devour' [through *fostering* **mental aberration**]: Whom resist steadfast in the faith, knowing that the same *afflictions* [prominent among those afflictions are **mental blindness**, or **lack of Insight**] are accomplished in your brethren that are in the world. I Peter 5:8, 9

> We are of God: he that knows God hears us; he that is not of God hears not us. Hereby know we The Spirit of Truth, and **the [demonic] spirit of error [in one's thinking and philosophy].** I John 4:6

---

[1]Most cultures of the world grant a prominent role to spirits in their world views. Throughout **Asia**, **Africa**, the **Pacific Islands**, and elsewhere in the non-Western world, the belief in evil spirits continues to be an integral part of the world view of many people groups.

Historically, we are, in fact, the anomaly. The last 300 years in the West represent the _only_ time in human history when the existence of evil spirits has been treated with wide-spread skepticism [due primarily to a philosophy of Rationalism, which denies the need to resort to spiritual explanations].

Nearly everyone living in **the Mediterranean world** during the Old and New Testament eras would have believed in the real existence of good and evil spirits.

In the first century, the **Jews, Greeks, Romans, Anatolians** (of Asia Minor), and **Egyptians** [some of the _most intelligent_ people to have ever lived] **all** believed spirits populated the heavens, underworld, and the earth.

Rather than questioning the existence of this realm, people sought ways to control the spirits and _to protect themselves_ from the sometimes dreadful workings of these spirits through ritual means.

A Collision of Worlds: Evil Spirits Then and Now, 2009

by Clinton E. Arnold, Ph.D., _Chairman and Professor. Department of New Testament Talbot School of Theology, Biola University, La Mirada, CA_

Published by C.S. Lewis Institute in their _Knowing & Doing_ teaching quarterly. Available on-line at:

http://www.cslewisinstitute.org/A_Collision_of_Worlds_FullArticle

The international community of mental health professionals **now** recognizes that science cannot categorically rule out potential spirit (or, what is known as _para-normal)_ involvement on every psychiatric issue, and, therefore, includes a diagnostic category labelled

'Trance and Possession Disorder'

as listed in the World Health Organization's

standard diagnostic manual

known as the

International Classification of Disease,

Version 10 (ICD-10).

It is also listed as a diagnostic entity within the American Psychiatric Association's (APA) _Diagnostic and Statistical Manual of Mental Disorders,_ Edition IV.

Area of Vulnerability or Concern	Troubling Thought
Personal Salvation	I don't think I am _really_ saved! I can't _ever_ be sure I am saved! I can _never_ be 'good enough' to be saved! Who am I to think I could be saved!
God's Unconditional Love	God doesn't _really_ love me! There is <u>no way</u> God could really love me! (For what I have done!) God may love others, but not me! I am completely unlovable!
The 'Unpardonable' Sin (also known as the _'Unforgiveable Sin'_, or the _'blasphemy <u>against</u> the Holy Spirit'_)	I _believe_ I have committed the unpardonable sin! My sins have been <u>so bad</u> I cannot be forgiven! I just know that I am doomed!
Severity (or number) of one's sins	It is too late for me! I am simply a 'lost' soul! I can never change! I haven't the power to change!
Pressure of trials	I can't take it anymore! I am going to 'give up'! I cannot wait for deliverance any longer! I am defeated!

Area of Vulnerability or Concern	Troubling Thought
Mental Stability or Sanity	I think I am losing my mind! I fear I am going insane! I'm going to have a nervous breakdown! (I can't handle life!) I can no longer control my thinking! My feelings control me!
Demon Possession	I belong to the devil! An evil spirit is going to harm me! I am powerless before demons! I am afraid (terrified) of demons! I am in terrible danger from demons!
Physical (or *Mental*) Healing	I can't (and *won't*) be healed! I don't believe I <u>can</u> be healed! I lack the faith to be healed! Healing is not in the Atonement! (*That* was for another time and place!) Healing is not meant for me!
Forgiveness of Sin	Have I <u>overlooked</u> confessing some sin? Have I been *contrite* enough when I confessed this sin? Have I spent *sufficient* time in enumerating my sins? (Or, was I too hasty in doing so?) What if my sins are not forgiven?

Religious Scrupulosity, you recall, pertains to unwarranted, inappropriate, obsessional, <u>over</u>-concern in religious matters detrimental to one's peace.

There are four types of demonic interaction. They are: *demon influenced, demon afflicted, demon oppressed,* and *demon possessed.* The areas of bodily contact are also four, respectively corresponding to the four types of interaction. And, finally, there are four kinds of demon manifestation corresponding to the four types of interaction, as well.

The first type of demon interaction is: *demon influenced.* Here, the OCPD person experiences relatively mild discomfort as the spirit influences (harmful thought impressions) *impinge* upon the person's physically **external**, bio-electric energy field which surrounds the human form. This kind of mind manifestation originates outside the person's body entirely, yet is strong enough to influence thought and feeling negatively.

The second type of demon interaction is: *demon afflicted.* The affliction can be physical or emotional, and intermittent. Here, discomfort symptoms range from moderate to severe, occurring **internal** to the OCPD person's bio-electric energy field (yet still external to the physical body). This kind of emotional/physical manifestation may take numerous forms involving multiple 'psyche' disruptions and body malfunctions.

The third type of demon interaction is: *demon oppressed.* Here, the emotional and physical realms display extreme upset or stress, where there is a clear danger to emotional/physical health either immediately, or building (usually quickly) over time. This takes place within the OCPD person's heart-generated bio-electric energy field internal to the physical body. Oppression takes many forms, highly turbulent, volatile.

The fourth type of demon interaction is: *demon possessed.* Here, the OCPD person's 'will' is compromised, and the evil spirit actually inhabits the OCPD person's mind. The unclean spirit has full control.

(See *corresponding table* on next page for a correlation of all the above)

Types of Demonic Interaction, Area of Bodily Contact, and Kinds of Manifestation an OCPD Person Will Likely Experience Who *Succumbs*

Type of Interaction	Area of Contact	Kind of Manifestation
1 Demon Influenced (mental) *Mild* discomfort **NOTE:** OCPD people are clearly <u>more</u> susceptible than *non*-OCPD people	External to a person's distinct and unique, heart-generated bio-electric energy field (or body aura), yet close enough to impact it with harmful thought impressions.	This kind of mind manifestation originates **outside** of the person <u>entirely</u>, yet is strong enough to *influence* thought and *suggest* unwise, hurtful, characteristic OCPD choices.
2 Demon *Afflicted* (emotional and/or physical) can be intermittent *Moderate* to <u>severe</u> discomfort **NOTE**: Again, OCPD people <u>more</u> susceptible due to their **predominantly negative state**	*Within* a person's <u>outer</u> bio-electric energy field (external to the physical body), extending *from* the physical body several feet in all directions. (Such a **negatively charged field** *attracts* negative entities)	OCPD affliction may take form as nervousness and upset; bodily maladies, such as skin eruptions and itching, temperature fluctuations, impaired breathing, sound and light sensitivity, sleep disturbances, insomnia, easily startled.
3 **Demon Oppressed** (emotional **and** physical) <u>Extreme</u> upset **Danger** to physical health of oppressed (over time) *or* to the person interacting, both a distinct <u>possibility</u> **NOTE**: Here, OCPD traits can be **magnified** to the *maximal* degree possible	*Within* a person's heart-generated *inner* bio-electric energy field (internal to the physical body) permeating every member and organ of the entire physical body. (The mind being immaterial, or *non*-physical, is excepted.) (Here, the interpenetrating **negative energy life field** attracts directly – *into* the flesh – malevolent entities, and/or their energies)	Oppression may take the form of *highly* turbulent, volatile emotions, such as **fiery** anger and arguing, **tremendously** accusing, **strong** resentment, **great** frustration, **very high** levels of dissatisfaction, **extreme** criticalness, **forceful** domination, **ugly** facial grimacing, **loud** shouting, cursing, **totally** unreasoning and illogical.
4 **Demon Possessed** (of OCPD will or volition) *Unbelievable* torment	Inhabiting a person's mind or **mental body** (also called the 'Inner Man', 'Inner Person' or psyche) It is in full control.	Shaking, epileptic fits, mouth frothing, deafness, blindness, muteness, self-mutilate. <u>Extremely rare</u>![1]

[1]Other extremes: face contorting, voice change, eyes change color/glow, unnatural strength

Types of Demonic Interaction, Area of Bodily Contact, and Kinds   31
Manifestation a _Non_-OCPD Person Can Experience
(Due to _regular_ <u>close</u> association with an OCPD Person)

Type of <u>Interaction</u>	Area of <u>Contact</u>	Kind of <u>Manifestation</u>
1 Demon Influenced (mental) _Mild_ discomfort _(if any)_	External to a person's distinct and unique, heart-generated bio-electric energy field (or body aura) yet close enough to impact it with harmful thought impressions.	This kind of mind manifestation originates **outside** of the person <u>entirely</u>, yet is strong enough to _influence_ thought and _suggest_ unwise, hurtful choices.
2		
Demon Afflicted (emotional and/or physical), can be intermittent Moderate discomfort to <u>borderline</u> severe	_Within_ a person's <u>outer</u> bio-electric energy field (external to the physical body), extending _from_ the physical body several feet in all directions.	Affliction may take the form of nervousness and upset; bodily maladies, such as skin eruptions and itching, temperature fluctuations, headaches, stomach distress.
3		
Demon Oppressed (emotional **and** physical), Severe discomfort or impairment, **Danger** to life and limb of oppressed, _or_ to another a <u>real</u> likelihood	_Within_ a person's heart-generated _inner_ bio-electric energy field (internal to the physical body) permeating every member and organ of the entire physical body. (The mind being immaterial, or _non_-physical, is excepted)	Oppression may take the form of distressing bodily ailments, such as breathing or allergy problems **_greatly_** magnified, often the non-OCPD person will become loud and shout when arguing with the OCPD person, uncharacteristically.
4		
Demon Possessed (will or volition), pure, absolute, psycho-physical pain) _Unremitting_ torment	Inhabiting a person's mind or **mental body**. Person may be _totally unconscious_ of their situation while possessed.	If the _non_-OCPD person is fairly well balanced (has <u>no</u> mental illness of any kind), chance of this is practically **non-existent.**

(All Gospel verses bestowing Power and Authority over)

Matt. 10:1 And when he had called unto him his twelve disciples, he gave them power against unclean spirits, **to cast them out,** and to heal all manner of sickness and all manner of disease.

Matt. 10:7, 8 *And as ye go, preach, saying, The kingdom of heaven is at hand. Heal the sick, cleanse the lepers, raise the dead, **cast out devils:** freely ye have received, freely give.*

Matt. 28:19, 20 *Go ye therefore, and teach all nations, baptizing them in the name of the Father, and of the Son, and of the Holy Ghost:* Teaching them to **observe all things** *[includes <u>casting</u> <u>out</u> demons]* **whatsoever I have commanded you:** *and, lo, I am with you alway, even unto the end of the world.* Amen.

Mark 3:14, 15 And he ordained twelve, that they should be with him, and that he might send them forth to preach, and to have power to heal sicknesses, and to **cast out devils:**

Mark 16:15, 17 And he said unto them, *Go ye into all the world, and preach the gospel to every creature. And* these signs shall follow <u>**them that believe**</u>*; **In my name shall they cast out devils; they shall speak with new tongues;***

Luke 9:1, 2 Then he called his twelve disciples together, and [he] gave them **power and authority over all devils,** and to cure diseases. And he sent them to preach the kingdom of God, and to heal the sick.

Luke 10:17-20 And the seventy returned again with joy, saying, Lord, even **the devils are subject unto us through thy name.** And he said unto them, *I beheld Satan as lightning fall from heaven. Behold, **I give unto you power to tread on serpents and scorpions,** and over all the power of the enemy: and nothing shall by any means hurt you. Notwithstanding in this rejoice not, that **the spirits are <u>subject</u> unto you;** but rather rejoice, because your names are written in heaven.*

(Note the **Great Commission** (final) directive from Jesus pertains to *'them that[shall]believe'*[**you** and **me**]. See *next* three pages for display presentation)

Jesus' <u>Official</u> Conferral of Authority
on the Believer to Subdue and Banish Demons

'Behold,

I give unto YOU

[faithful followers of my Person and Name]

P O W E R

[<u>Authority</u> original Greek]

to tread on *serpents* and *scorpions*,

[Jesus' terms for demons]

AND – over ALL the power

of the enemy

[Satan the Devil]:

and **nothing**

[***NO*** fallen angel, <u>no</u> <u>matter</u> their rank]

shall by <u>any</u> means hurt you

[in your *administering* of <u>this</u> Authority]'

Gospel of Luke – *Authorized Document*
Chapter 10, Verse 19

'Go ye therefore

[you Twelve Apostles],

and teach all nations,

teaching *them*

[those <u>future</u> Christians, YOU reading this document]

to observe ALL things

whatsoever I have commanded you

[among them,

'In my Name [**YOU**] *<u>shall</u>* cast out devils'],

and, lo, I am with you always,

even unto the end of the world.

[or, the Age]'

Gospel of Matthew – *Authorized Document*

Chapter 10, Verse 8; **Chapter 16,** Verse 17;
and **Chapter 28,** Verses 19, 20

Jesus' <u>Official</u> Conferral of Authority
on the Believer to Subdue and Banish Demons – *Con.*

'And when He

had called unto Him

His twelve disciples, He gave them **Power**

<u>against</u> unclean spirits

to <u>cast</u>

<u>them</u> out,

And the seventy returned again with joy,

saying, Lord,

even the devils

are **subject** unto us

through

<u>**Thy**</u> **[Invincible] Name.**'

Gospels of Matthew and Luke – *Authorized Document*
Chapter 10, Verse 1**; Chapter 10**, Verse 17,
respectively

Mini-Prayers to Expel OCPD Demons
In the *Invincible* Name of Jesus!
And by the **Power** of His *shed* Life's Blood*, I **stand** *against* you, demons, and I **command** you, by the **Authority** vested in me by my Saviour, to *cease* and *desist* harassing _____ who suffers from OCPD, and I **command** you to release your hold on _____ , *now!* Amen!
New Frontier Health Research Copyright ©2015

Mini-Prayers to Expel OCPD Demons
In the *Invincible* Name of Jesus!
And by the **Power** of His *precious shed Blood!* I **command** you, unclean spirits, to *flee* from _____'s presence, as **the Spirit of God** claims _____ wholly, *as His own!* You have **NO Power** here, any longer, to either *cause* or exacerbate his/her OCPD! Amen!
New Frontier Health Research Copyright ©2015

Mini-Prayers to Expel OCPD Demons
In the *Invincible* Name of Jesus!
And by the **Unassailable Merits** of His Atonement on the Cross for _____ , I **command** you, demons, to *loose* _____ from your evil clutches, and *remove* from his/her mind whatever OCPD lies and falsehoods you have planted there! In Christ's Name! Amen!
New Frontier Health Research Copyright ©2015

Mini-Prayers to Expel Demons
In the *Invincible* Name of Jesus!
And by *His* **Victory** over all the forces of evil at Calvary' Hill, I **command** you to *remove* yourselves from _____'s *Life energy field*, which surrounds him/her, and be *repelled* from it, forevermore! The **Power** of God **shatters** your hold on _____ this instant! Amen!
New Frontier Health Research Copyright ©2015

Mini-Prayers to Expel OCPD Demons
In the *Invincible* Name of Jesus!
And by the Wonder-Working **Power** of *Jesus'* *shed* blood*! I command you, demon's of Satan, to be **hurled** far and wide from _____ , whom you have mercilessly *oppressed* with OCPD, and never return to afflict him/her ever again! In the Saviour's Name! Amen!
New Frontier Health Research Copyright ©2015

Mini-Prayers to Expel OCPD Demons
In the *Invincible* Name of Jesus!
And by *His* Authority over all angelic forces, I **command** you, demons, to *leave* _____ , *forevermore!* Further, I **order** you to *withdraw* all influence you have exerted upon _____ for ill, and *never again* seek to dominate _____'s life, **nor** enable his/her OCPD! Amen!
New Frontier Health Research Copyright ©2015

Mini-Prayers to Expel OCPD Demons
In the *Invincible* Name of Jesus!
And by the 'All-Power' He wields from Heaven, to **compel** you, through the **Authority** granted me, to *come out* of _____ and release him/her from the prison of OCPD torment and fear! Depart, *now!* And be *banished* from _____'s presence! Amen!
New Frontier Health Research Copyright ©2015

Mini-Prayers to Expel Demons
In the *Invincible* Name of Jesus!
And by the **Supreme Love** of the Father for _____ , I **command** you, evil spirits, to *vacate* this body temple of _____'s, and, thereby, *restore* him/her to complete mental and emotional normalcy! Your oppression of _____ is ended, *now!* By Christ's Word! Amen!
New Frontier Health Research Copyright ©2015

Mini-Prayers to Expel OCPD Demons
In the *Invincible* Name of Jesus!
And by the **Resurrection Power** He wields, I **command** you, fallen ones, to *rush away* from _____'s person, and *take with you* all OCPD traits and tendencies you have encouraged and fostered within him/her, never to nurture again! In Jesus' Name! Amen!
New Frontier Health Research Copyright ©2015

Mini-Prayers to Expel OCPD Demons
In the *Invincible* Name of Jesus!
And by the **Authority** bestowed upon me as a **true** follower of the Living Christ, I **command** all evil entities who are afflicting _____ to *come out* of him/her! And know he/she is a 'chosen vessel' to which you can *never* harm again! By Christ Command, Amen!
New Frontier Health Research Copyright ©2015

While there are **many signs** which indicate a person is the object of demonic attention, there are only **three broad**, yet *distinct*, **categories of signs** as follows: signs of influence, direction, and control.

Under the first category, Signs of Influence, the operating *interface* between demons and the human is the *medium of* **emotions**. This researcher has identified no fewer than nineteen negative *emotional* groupings (including associated bodily sensations) which fall within this feeling realm: Lack of inner peace, negative feelings, unforgivingness and bitterness, insomnia, helplessness, dissatisfied criticalness, ungratefulness and disrespect, fear and anxiety, feelings of inadequacy and worthlessness (low self-esteem), aversion *to* the Scriptures, discomfort *with* the Scriptures, feelings of weariness relative to prayer, feelings of incompleteness or of not-being-as-good-as (inferiority complex), feelings that one must be 'perfect' (perfection complex), feelings of being permanently damaged and irreparably violated (a victim complex), feelings of anger, even rage (an anger complex), feelings of guilt, shame, and of being to blame, jittery and easily startled, and, lastly, feelings of losing, or having lost, control as in having the impulse to 'run away', scream, or to 'lash out' at another.

Under the second category, Signs of Direction, the operating interface between demons and the human is the *medium of* **thought**. This researcher has identified, again, no fewer than nineteen negative *thought* groupings which fall within the mental realm: unwanted, intrusive thoughts; repetitive, unwelcome thoughts; thoughts contrary to one's moral code; unwholesome, unnatural, and unhealthful thoughts; bizarre, frightful dreams; disturbing or sacrilegious images; energy-draining, 'depolarized' thoughts; distorted concept of God; false self-concept; misreads motives and intentions of others; attracted to the supernatural; entertains wrong concept of Life's Purpose; fearful of the status of one's salvation; believes one's self to be basically evil; a continual focus on the 'bad'; drawn to non-edifying topics involving baser human behaviors; expresses errant thoughts to others without 'screening' them; envisions the worst outcome; and having the urge to commit to writing errant (offensive) thoughts.

Under the third category, Signs of Control, the operating interface between demons and the human is the *medium of* **direct intervention**. Identified, again, are no fewer than nineteen negative *direct intervention* groupings which fall within the mental *and* physical realms: eating disorders and dietary imbalances; reluctance (even fear) to defecate; extreme fatigue not relieved by sleep; extreme sensitivity to light, sound, odor, temperature, even touch; unusual, strange, or untreatable (unresponsive) skin problems; hears voices others do not hear; self-mutilates, burns, or bruises oneself; participates in satanic rituals, sometimes in the nude; holds to a perverted, or unwholesome, view of sex; slave to sexual fantasies and masturbation; held captive to major obsessions/compulsions to the point of being 'possessed'; labors under a powerful addition (often multiple), such as drugs or pornography; experiences sudden outbursts of emotion out of proportion to the precipitating factor; unable to heal where treatments are usually effective; experiences multiple sclerosis symptoms of tremors and shaking; blinded to reception of Truth; endures recurring headaches; experiences dizziness often; and suffers with pain body-wide.

NOTE: In this last category, these malevolent entities seem to be able to *alter* or *manipulate* the various bodily systems, such as the circulatory system, the nervous system, the endocrine system, the temperature regulating system, the digestive system, the excretory system, the energy regulating system, the reproductive system, the auditory system, and the olfactory system. Also, these physical disturbances often prove totally enigmatic to physicians because the root causes often cannot be found.

(See *corresponding table* on next page for a correlation of all the above)

(Columns read down)

Signs of Influence (Medium is _emotions_)	Signs of Direction (Medium is _thought_)	Signs of **Control** (Medium is _direct intervention_)
1		
Lack of inner peace	Unwanted, intrusive thoughts	Eating disorders (anorexia, bulimia) or dietary imbalances
2		
Negative feelings	Repetitive, unwelcome thoughts	Reluctance to defecate (may require 'surgical' intervention)
3		
Unforgiving and bitter	Thoughts contrary, in direct opposition, to your personal moral code	Extreme fatigue
4		
Insomnia (due to upset emotions, worry)	Your attention is _drawn_ to _un_wholesome, _un_natural, and _un_healthful things in conflict with your true desires	Extreme sensitivity to light, sound (and/or volume), odor, temperature, even touch
5		
Feel helpless to change	Experiencing bizarre, frightful dreams	Unusual, or strange, skin problems
6		
Critical (_feels_ great dissatisfaction)	Experiencing disturbing (even sacrilegious) images	Hears voices (or refuses to listen to, _discuss_, harsh aspects of reality)
7		
Ungrateful and disrespectful	Negative, energy-draining, 'depolarized' thought	Self-mutilates, burns, or bruises oneself
8		
Fearful and anxious	**Distorted** concept of God	Satanic ritual participant
9		
Low self-esteem (_feels_ inadequate, worthless)	False self-concept (one's **true Identify** in Christ is **unknown**)	Perverted view of sex and/or sexual aberrations
10		
Reluctant to **read/recite Scripture** (_feel_ it is punishing, accusing, or corrective) or **attend church**	Severe perceptual problems regarding others' motives or actions; easily _mis_-read or _mis_-interpret intentions	Preoccupied with, and/or a slave to, masturbation
11		
Uncomfortable w/ Scripture	Drawn to the supernatural	_(Continued on next page)_

Signs of Influence	Signs of Direction	Signs of **Control**
Reluctant to **pray** (*feel* it is too much work, tiresome, tedious, or of no use) 12	Wrong concept of Life's Purpose, believe one is meant to suffer, and/or bound by fate	Major mental obsessions/ compulsions (to the point of *seeming* to be 'possessed')
13		
Possesses inferiority complex (*feel* inadequate, lacking, incomplete, not-as-good)	Question one's salvation, or believes one is 'lost' or is 'doomed', or will be 'damned'	Addictions (drugs, alcohol, food, intercourse, illicit sex, pornography, etc.)
14		
Possesses perfection complex (*feel* one must strive to be 'perfect', else one is a failure)	Believes one is 'evil', or is a child of the devil	Sudden (even violent) outbursts of emotion (illogical and irrational)
15		
Possesses a 'victim' complex (*feel* helpless, powerless, permanently violated)	One's continual *mental focus* is on the hurtful, the harmful, or on the bad	Inability to heal (though one may pray *earnestly* for healing, and take medications)
16		
Possesses an anger complex (*feels* justified in being angry, and *feels* the need to punish another)	Listens to, reads, or watches, videos, DVD's, TV broad- casts, internet presentations on non-edifying topics involv- ing baser human behaviors	Multiple sclerosis **symptoms** (abnormal sensations, such as tingling, crawling, or burning) tremors, muscle weakness, trouble swallowing
17		
Guilty and to blame, feel shameful	Errant thoughts are articu- lated to others without censure	Blinded to reception of Truth and to one's own faults
18		
Jittery and startles easily	Envision the worst to occur	Headaches (very common)
19		
Feels will lose control, will run away, and scream	Mentally urged to commit to writing errant thoughts	Vertigo (dizziness) (very com)
		Pain body-wide (very common)

NOTE: These signs (or traits) **may** either *originate* from demonic sources (having been 'planted' by them in either your mind or heart, and/or these traits will most certainly *invite* and *encourage* demonic oversight and control. The latter is because one's thought vibrations and emotional frequency is then 'tuned-in' to the frequency of malevolent entities. The frequencies resonate with each other, and consequently, information (in the form of ideas and suggestions) may readily 'flow' between both parties, and be easily and readily exchanged, even unbeknown to yourself. **It should be noted that the <u>more</u> of these traits a person possesses, including their degree of *forcefulness*, the <u>greater</u> the likelihood that malevolent intelligences are at work in their lives.** Recognize, too, that the three mediums of influence, direction, and control may 'overlap' into each other, as well. Although, these hurtful, harmful, traits listed above do *primarily* fall within these three respective 'degrees' of human/demonic interaction/interchange.

There are numerous *unusual* perceptible signs often quite evident to both the OCPD person and to the non-OCPD person that demonic activity is underway in association with the OCPD person. Other signs exist, but the following is a list of subjective and objective observances the author has had first-hand experience with relative to several OCPD people he has personally known that are frequent and prominent ones:

Experienced by the OCPD Person

1. The OCPD person may relate to another that from time-to-time they have the **_sense_** there is another 'person' in their room, when, in fact, they are the ONLY person in the room. This can occur in the middle of the night, or, *equally as often*, in broad daylight.

2. The OCPD person may tell of their **'hearing'** the sound of someone walking throughout their home, the tell-tale sound of *presumably* human footsteps, when, in fact, no other 'person' is in their home at the time.

3. The OCPD person may share that they frequently have 'bad', unsettling dreams, which are disjointed in content, and often <u>cannot</u> be clearly recalled. However, their disquieting effect lingers in their mind.

4. The OCPD person may **'catch a glimpse'** out of the *corner of their eye* (their peripheral vision) of what they perceive to be a 'person', but upon turning in that direction, see nothing.

5. The OCPD person may <u>feel</u> *unusually uncomfortable*, especially if left alone, for no discernible, logical reason, and may request that you stay with them till that feeling passes.

6. The _non_-OCPD person, a sibling, parent, adult child, friend, or acquaintance, may _sense_ **strongly**, particularly after a time of repeated interaction with the OCPD person, that 'something is amiss' with this person (psycho-spiritually) speaking, even though the _non_-OCPD person has **no** understanding of OCPD, and in fact, possesses **no** knowledge of OCPD, at all.

7. The _non_-OCPD person may, all at once, be suddenly struck by the fact that the OCPD person seems to be speaking, reciting nonsensical arguments, in a wholly **'unconscious'** manner. As though the OCPD person were actually _profoundly_ unaware of the absurdity, irrationality, and non-advisability of their arguments, which, indeed, they are.

8. The _non_-OCPD person may detect that the OCPD person is _not_ in full, conscious control of themselves, in that they have _not_ the _slightest inkling_ they are engaging in vocal behavior, speech patterns, and the like, that reveal their utter **bondage** to fallacious ideas and notions, evidenced by their greatly _strained_ facial expressions and _distressed_ speech.

9. The _non_-OCPD person may see _reflected_ in the OCPD person's pet, such as a cat or dog, behaviors which are uncharacteristic of that species, such as uncalled-for and exaggerated fear reactions, enduring and persistent nervous behaviors, and habits which are detrimental to the animals well-being, such as 'staring fixations', 'pacing in circles', unusual howlings, and acting as though there were _other_ individuals in a given room, when in fact, there are no other people in the room. This type of abnormal animal behavior is often evidenced by the pet looking _intently_ in one direction, down a hall, into a corner, etc., and in the case of a canine, barking or

growling as they do so. (Interestingly, veterinarians are <u>stymied</u> 43 by these behaviors and label them as 'canine cognitive dysfunction' or 'canine senility'!) The poor creature may even develop erratic eating and toileting habits, to the point of <u>refusing</u> to take a daily walk, and be reluctant, and even refuse, to defecate – *for days.*

10.   The <u>*non*</u>-OCPD person may observe a continual deterioration of natural, healthy, normal behavior by the OCPD person, and even a physical deterioration of their health, though slowly, gradually, yet steadily, over time, again, for no readily discernable reason.

These observances can **all** be signs demonic activity is present and underway. And, when <u>*several*-*to*-*numerous*</u> of these characteristics are found together, there's hardly any doubt, some degree of demonic presence and influence is being exerted, and is being experienced by the OCPD sufferer.

Some other miscellaneous occurrences may involve recurring feelings of being 'watched', believing that objects in the OCPD person's house are being re-arranged, or misplaced, <u>*of themselves*</u>, and even the experiencing of unusual odors.

Lastly, extreme sensitivity to sound, hyper-sensitivity to light, and heightened sensitivity to smells, can also, occur.

What this Situation Responsibly Calls For

The OCPD person, and *even their pet*, need to have recited over them (if the OCPD person is open to this procedure) **a ritual of demonic expulsion**. Fortunately, this does <u>not</u> require the services, necessarily, of any ecclesiastical authority versed in these matters. However, on occasion, resorting to expertise of an experienced 'exorcist' would be prudent should the <u>*non*</u>-OCPD person lack confidence in their ability to perform it. Also, you CAN perform an exorcism <u>*apart*</u> from the OCPD person's knowledge, if need be. **Although, It should <u>not</u> be undertaken by a Christian <u>lacking</u> in protection belief afforded by the Scriptures.**

Beliefs which Protect the Christian

1. As a committed believer in Jesus Christ, a 'born-from-above' Christian, I am invulnerable (**cannot** be harmed) by <u>any</u> demon, or league of demons, in the practice of exorcism.

2. As a faithful follower of Jesus Christ, I can speak to the demons **boldly** and **confidently**, knowing they MUST (are compelled) by God's Power to heed my words.

3. As a devoted disciple of Jesus Christ, I can **know** with certainty that <u>any</u> demons I address are **subject** to my command, though they may, predictably, exhibit reluctance to obey.

4. As a disciplined soldier of Jesus Christ, I bear the mantle of the **Authority** of Jesus on my person, and can speak to demons **in** that inviolate (*<u>cannot</u>* be countermanded) Authority.

5. As a humble servant of Jesus Christ, I can **DEMAND** that demons <u>depart</u> from any person who sincerely repents of their departures from the Law of Love, *<u>and</u>* who is dedicated to living for the Lord.

6. As a consecrated priest (in God's eyes) of Jesus Christ, I have the *very* **Righteousness** of Christ, *Himself*, <u>imputed</u> to me (reckoned to my credit), to which the Devil, nor his demons, <u>cannot</u> accuse.

7. As a royal king (in God's eyes) directly under Jesus Christ, I can issue **ORDERS** directly to demons, and they are constrained to **obey**, though they may scream, shout, and protest the whole time.

8. As a **Free-Born** Child of the **Living God**, and a **true** brother or sister to Jesus Christ, I have about me **angelic hosts** assigned to me for my added protection, as well. Therefore, I need have **NO FEAR**!

Let it be crystal clear that malevolent spiritual entities need <u>never</u> be feared as long as one is 'under the mantle' of the Lord Jesus Christ. His atoning sacrifice on the Cross two millennia ago, *totally* and *permanently* defeated **all** spiritual creatures of rebellion against God. For we are told in Holy Scripture that Jesus '**spoiled** principalities and powers [**all** of them], he made a shew of them openly [a public humiliating exhibition], **triumphing over them** in It [The *Atoning Work* of the **Cross**]'. (Colossians 2:15) And, though these creatures are still permitted to 'rule' this world, their control of it has been considerably curtailed (thanks be to God!), and is destined to utterly cease.

Still, today, all people (even Christians) have to contend with their malicious influence, which they can *still* impart to unsuspecting humans who 'open the door' to their entrance whenever they indulge in arrogant and presumptuous thinking and loveless behaviors.

<u>Here are two Scriptural renditions to confirm this</u>:

'For we do *not* wrestle against flesh and blood, but against principalities, against powers, against the rulers of the darkness of this world, against spiritual hosts [old English for '<u>armies</u>'] of **wickedness** in the heavenly place [or high places]' (KJV, Ephesians 6:12), and again,

'For our wrestling match is *not* against 'persons with bodies' [rather those beings *without* physical bodies] but against rulers with various areas and descending orders of authority, against the **world dominators** of the *present* **darkness**.' (Derek Prince version, Ephesians 6:12).

Be that as it may, we, as 'children of The Light' can exercise all the <u>**Commanding Authority**</u> Christ has bequeathed to us to **expel** demonic 'strongholds' in our, and our OCPD loved one's, mind and heart. For all of our sakes, let us <u>not</u> be found negligent, or cowering, in doing so!

A Master Tool to *Inspire*

INSIGHT

(that priceless treasure that can set you free)

The Twenty-Third Psalm

for the OCPD Person

The Lord's Prayer

for the OCPD Person

Message of Isaiah 43

to the OCPD Person

by Mack W. Ethridge

The Judeo-Christian Hebrew and Greek Scriptures, known collectively as the Holy Bible, contain passages of such Heart-Convicting **Power** and **Persuasiveness**, as to have <u>no equal</u> in the realm of literature, ancient or modern. No less will *these* words, resting upon their foundation, bring YOU **Insight**, if only you open yourself to them. Read each of them, and ponder them, daily, and begin to have them **transform** your thinking and feeling worlds for your highest and best good.

The Lord is my shepherd, I shall not want.

He maketh me to grow in **Insight**;

He leadeth me into relationships where I become more **aware**

of my desire to control, criticize, and complain, so I might _extinguish_ it.

He restoreth **wholeness** and **normalcy** to my soul.

He leadeth me in the paths of **correct** and **positive thinking**

for His name's sake, and for my liberation from _extreme orderliness,_

perfectionism, enslavement to rules, inflexible attitudes,

and _tyrannical_ and _judgmental practices._

Yea, though I walk through the valley of my life-diminishing feelings,

I will fear them not, for Thou art with me to _transmute_ them.

Thy **Truth statements** and meditations, they comfort me,

as they _correct_ my misperceptions, and abandon _over conscientiousness._

Thou preparest a table before me in the presence of

my sincere, yet _erroneous_ thinking and mistaken viewpoints.

Thou anointest my head with the oil of **discernment**

and the _willingness_ to acknowledge and embrace the Truth.

My cup of Truth is filling up more and more.

Surely patience and thoughtfulness and sensitivity toward others' **rights**

to **self-determination** shall follow me all the days of my life,

and I will dwell in the house of goodwill actions, respectful acceptance,

and **rescuing Sanity**, forever.

Our Father, Who art in Heaven,

Hallowed be Thy name.

Thy Kingdom come, Thy will be done,

On earth, as it is in Heaven.

Give us this day our daily bread of **Insight** into our _faulty_ interpretations of Reality, so that our relationships might be harmonious and just.

And forgive us our trespasses against those persons we have _disrespected_ by denying them *their right to choose* their own way,

As we forgive those OCPD persons who trespass against us by _their_ attempts to curtail _our_ rights to self-direction and un-coerced decision.

And lead us not into the temptation to think our knowing better, or believing to know better, about any given subject authorizes us to _impose_ our views or methods
on others,

But deliver us from this constellation of dishonoring evils.

For Thine is the Kingdom

(_not_ ours, to _dictate_ or _demand_),

And the power, and the glory,

Forever.

Amen.

Do Not Be Afraid

Do not be afraid, for I have redeemed you from the blindness and senselessness of denying you have OCPD.

I have called you by your name; you are mine.

When you walk through the obscuring waters of misperception, I will be with you to <u>correct</u> them, and give you true perception, instead;

You will never sink beneath these waves.

When the fire of your inflamed feelings of anger and control, criticism and judgment, is burning all around you,

You will never be consumed by these flames.

When the fear of *your* loneliness, which <u>*you*</u> have created by driving others away from you through their mistreatment and disrespect of their persons and rights, is looming,

Then remember I am at your side.

You are mine, O my child; I am your Father,

And I love you with a perfect love that will _transform_ you, and *heal* you, and *deliver* you from your negative, compulsive, relationship-destroying traits, *as you yield to Me* – and obey. Amen.

✝

But Jesus

Beheld Them,

And Said Unto Them,

With Men This Is Impossible;

<u>But</u>

With God

ALL Things

[even the **<u>Curing</u>** of OCPD]

Are Possible!

Matthew 19:26

(Adapted)

Dear Friends of New Frontier Health Research,

This book is meant to be an Inspiration to all OCPD sufferers, where *before* there was no inspiration; an anchor of Hope, where *before* there was no hope that this disorder could ever be mastered. Hope and belief that OCPD <u>can</u> be overcome, <u>*Can*</u> be defeated, <u>CAN</u> be permanently banished from one's life! And I trust I have conveyed to you, the reader, the REALITY that this can be so! OCPD is NOT an incurable mental illness, *so long as one keeps the living God in the picture!* God, in His Mercy, Grace, and Power, and in His **Divine Revelation** from which Insights may flow, constitutes the missing piece to the puzzle of Insight for the OCPD sufferer. Insights that are based, not on *faulty* assumptions about life, or 'broken' practices, but on Divine Truth which can take hold of one's heart and soul, and liberate the mind from the shackles of OCPD torment and fear!

With this book in hand, and with even the <u>tiniest</u> measure of Insight (as small as a grain of mustard seed!) and/or willingness to honestly explore the realm of your inner being, you **now** have the means to tackle the 'giant' of OCPD and the wherewithal to bring this giant crashing down to its knees! – With YOU being the clear and indisputable Victor over your world! If you are the person with OCPD, utilize every help within these pages to your advantage. Photocopy the reminder 'cards' of Truth pages, cut them out to business card size, and carry them with you to refresh your memory, and for times of special need. **Speak** the proclamations and declarations <u>*out loud,*</u> and with <u>emotional</u> <u>conviction</u> wherever and whenever possible, to convince your subconscious mind you mean business, and will settle for nothing less than total Victory over OCPD!

And lastly, recognize <u>YOU</u> have been graced with liberating psychological and **spiritual Knowledge** about Insight that <u>countless</u> OCPD sufferers don't have; making Freedom, your heritage as a beloved child of God, well within your reach! Therefore, know that my continuing prayer for you is that our great God will grant you **the Miracle of Insight!** Now, and <u>*forever more!*</u>

With Every Good Wish, and In Christ's Love, The Author

A DESTINED CLASSIC!

Original Disclosure!

Ground-breaking Volume!

When OCPD Meets the Power of God!

By **Mack W. Ethridge** *(See next page for details)*

Source Volume for OCPD

Bondage and Spiritual Warfare!

(*Expanded* Brochure)

The volume showcased on the previous page, *When OCPD Meets the* *Power of God!*, is already on its way to becoming a classic even though it was just introduced to the world last month. Witness to this fact is that of all the many people who are discovering this book, or those who have been asked to evaluate it, only the best of commendations are forthcoming, and only the highest of praise is being offered.

Therefore, the volume, *When OCPD Meets the Power of God*, is the perfect companion to the expanded brochure, *OCPD Bondage and Spiritual Warfare*, that you hold in your hand, because the vital content of this *latter* book was excerpted from the original source book, which contains little-known and much-needed information on the *remaining six of seven arenas* where blocks to 'Insight' arise.

Your education regarding the sources of OCPD lack of Insight will then be complete, with every known and proven step to freedom laid out before you, now – *well within your grasp!*

(Order your own copy of *'When OCPD Meets the Power of God!'* at Amazon.com, *today!*)

Romans 8:38

'For I am persuaded that neither death, nor life, *NOR* angels, *NOR* principalities, *NOR* powers, nor things present, nor things to come, nor height, nor depth, nor any other creature, shall be able to separate us from the Love of God, which is in Christ Jesus our Lord.'

Saint Paul

For *Immediate* Release (Apr. 2015)

By Authentic Life Publications

Book Review

By Mack Ethridge, founder of *Mercy Rose* Ministries Worldwide Outreach, and a leading recognized expert on ancient and modern Biblical Truth

---

ALP is proud to present an overview of a remarkable volume to have just recently appeared upon the spiritual/religious literary landscape! Yet, surely it is destined to have a profound impact! Entitled:

The Divine Plan Revealed!
– The Ultimate Revelation of Life's Purpose and God's Destiny for Man!

It sets forth The Glorious Gospel of Christ in Its Fullness! While most people are familiar with the elementary aspects of the Gospel Message, nearly all are ignorant of the more **mature**, *advanced* teachings of Scripture and of Christ.

This book provides in clear, concise, captivating language – designed for the layman – the following – and *much more!* And here are Truths seldom found under any one cover!

- Learn of aspects, glories, and Divine Truths about Jesus' person and teachings, which are either unknown, seldom taught, little understood, or misunderstood by His children, which will **Inspire you** and **Empower you** – *as no other teachings before!*
- Discover **the Truth about Riches, True Love,** and **the Great Universal Laws of Life**, if truly believed/lived, will bring fulfillment of your deepest heart's longing!
- Behold how you may live a **Life of Victory** and experience **The Joy of a Calm Spirit**, *in spite of your circumstances*, each and *every* day, through a surrendered life, and greater **Spiritual Knowledge!**
- Uncover The **Untold Mysteries of the Forgotten Cross**, undisclosed for hundreds of years, magnifying God's Love as *never* before!

- The **Hidden Glories of Our Lord's Resurrection**, unknown to much of the Christian world, and their profound significance
- What the '**Fullness** of the Gospel' really means, and _why_ so few people can scarcely believe it
- **The Greatest Discovery** ever made regarding the Heights and Depths of God's Love – _And_, Its **Breathtaking Implications!**
- The _Deeper_ Meaning of the '**Nativity Event**', and what the entrance of Divine Love into the world _really_ portended!
- The **Greatest** Single Achievement Christ will _ever_ have obtained, and the _Astonishing-Beyond-Belief,_ yet Wholly-True, Outcome!
- _Why_ people are **no longer astonished** at 'Christ's doctrine', as they virtually _always_ were, in early Christian eras!
- The _Unrealized Significance_ of **The Most Wonderful Words** ever spoken! – Bringing them alive as never before – _Today_!
- What the actual **Crusade of Jesus Christ** is all about, your _personal_ role in It, and **Its undreamed-of Outcome!**
- Hear **The Christ Tale _Never_ Told** to the world, which God desires to be told to all – _today!_
- The '**Hidden Dream**' cradled in the Saviour's Heart, a Dream few men or women have been made privy to, or privileged to hear!
- Obtain an accurate understanding of the major incidents of Jesus' Life, and the correct knowledge of **His Innermost Intentions** towards men!
- **The Greatest Lesson** our Lord desired **all** His followers to understand about His Cross, which tradition does _not_ speak to!
- Why you can **thrill** to the coming '**Dispensation of the Fullness of Times**' as spoken of by the Apostle Paul in his almost _ecstatic_ language – due to Its Unparalleled Majesty and Glory!
- New concepts/insights on **Healing**, which may be _precisely_ what you need to believe again for _deliverance of yourself **and** those you love and cherish!_

This 702-page **compendium** is the result of _a full twelve years_ of consecrated prayer, study, research, and contemplation, and subsequent Holy Spirit _'directed'_, commissioned writing, of Truths that have escaped the understanding of the Christian world. And is, also, the result of consulting highly reputable, respected sources going back to **1st Century A.D.**, and _before!_

A website dedicated to these teachings is under construction. Till then, this book can be ordered direct from www.Amazon.com   Thank you, God Bless!   **(4/15)**

(for psychological/physical healing and demonic oppression)

Chester and Betsy Kylstra, Founders

Restoring the Foundations (RTF) International
Hendersonville, North Carolina USA

828-696-9075
www.RestoringTheFoundations.org

Also, affiliated with the above-cited deliverance organization are Proclaiming His Word (PHW) Ministries, Inc.; Christian International (CI) Ministries; and Healing House Network of specially trained ministers.

Ministry teams of highly trained and qualified, committed individuals can be found within their ranks for your personal deliverance.

Henry and Donna Wright, Founders

Be in Health (an International organization)
Thomaston, Georgia USA

706-646-2074

Also, *Spiritual Lifeline*, 706-646-3600
www.beinhealth.com

This deliverance organization offers a number and variety of programs at their Be in Health campus, and conferences, worldwide.

(Above cited for informational purposes *only*. Reader assumes sole responsibility for contacting said parties, and holds the author blameless for any outcomes.)

How YOU Can Make a Difference in the Lives of OCPD People, their Co-Workers, and Their Loved Ones – Everywhere

— $ $ $ **COMPENSATION** *PROVIDED* $ $ $ —

The author's next book is going to be a collection of true life stories of *ordinary* people, such as you and I, who have discovered *extraordinary* ways (defined as 'ways that <u>WORK</u>!') to meet the challenge of OCPD, and to make definite headway in reclaiming a life of freedom: where cooperation, harmony, goodwill, joy, fulfillment, and peace predominate in all interpersonal relationships and their interactions, *exclusively* in the obsessive-compulsive realm.

The **first stage** of the project involves filling out a survey form (a questionnaire) relating to your OCPD situation: whether you have OCPD, or your friend or loved one; the particular traits you are having to contend with, the details of your relationship, and the like. Routine questions for the most part. (A pre-addressed, postage affixed envelope will be provided for your convenience.)

And, as a thank you, **<u>all</u> respondents** will be entitled to receive the author's monthly newsletter, Vibrant Hope, for a 6-month period, *free*.

Also, **anonymity will be ensured for those who desire it**, having their names and any identifying information changed (if included in the book).

Then, a section will be left wide open for you to share in *your own words* what approaches or methods you have unearthed which work for you and improve the quality of your relationship – in spite of OCPD tendencies and manifestations.

The **second stage** of the project will entail the author reviewing all the questionnaires and selecting those individuals who will be asked to be interviewed by phone (or in person, distance allowing). Should you accept, you will be compensated $25.00; *or* if you wish, receive a *complimentary* copy of the author's book, **OCPD's Only Hope of Psychological Wellness**, a $79.99 value.

Here is your chance to meet a vital, widely unaddressed, human need and be paid for your valuable time, experience, and goodwill.

Again, all responses will be keep strictly confidential (your personally identifiable information will *not* be shared with any third party), and all persons involved will remain anonymous should you so choose.

So, if you wish to help thousands of other OCPD affected people find ways to improve their lives, even *save* their lives, in some instances, please contact the author at one of the addresses listed below to request a questionnaire. (Be sure to include a postal mailing address.)

Your participation will go a long way in helping to free countless other people who have struggled, and are struggling, *daily*, with the cruel and relentless scourge of the mental disorder called OCPD.

Here are those addresses:

New Frontier Health Research

P.O. Box 1102

Waynesboro, VA 22980

Or

mackethridge@hotmail.com

Your **cooperation** is tremendously appreciated! Should you have questions, please don't hesitate to inquire at the above. Thank you sincerely, *M.W.E.*

OCPD Bondage and Spiritual Warfare!

Finis

(April 2015)

Selected Bibliography

(Pertaining to Spiritual Warfare *only*)

Biblical Healing and Deliverance, A Guide to Experiencing Freedom from Sins of the Past, Destructive Beliefs, Emotional & Spiritual Pain, Curses and Oppression, by Chester & Betsy Kylstra, published by Chosen Books, a Division of Baker Publishing Group, Minneapolis, Minnesota, 2014, www.chosenbooks.com, and www.RestoringTheFoundations.org

Spiritual Warfare, Jesus' Way, How to Conquer Evil Spirits & Live Victoriously, by Larry Richards, Ph.D., published by Chosen Books, A Division of Baker Publishing Group, Minneapolis, Minnesota, 2014

101 Answers to Questions About Satan, Demons, & Spiritual Warfare, by Mark Hitchcock, published by Harvest House Publishers, Eugene, Oregon, 2014, www.haresthousepublishers.com

An Insider's Guide to Spiritual Warfare, 30 Battle-Tested Strategies from Behind Enemy Lines, by Kristine McGuire, published by Chosen Books, a Division of Baker Publishing Group, Minneapolis, Minnesota, 2014, www.chosenbooks.com

The Full Armor of God, Defending Your Life from Satan's Schemes, by Larry Richards, published by Chosen Books, a Division of Baker Publishing Group, Minneapolis, Minnesota, 2013, www.chosenbooks.com

Prayers that Rout Demons & Break Curses, by John Eckhardt, published by Charisma House, Charisma House Book Group, Lake Mary, Florida, 2010, www.charismahouse.com

There's a Miracle in Your Mouth, If ye shall ask anything in My name, I will do it, by Don Gossett & E.W. Kenyon, published by Whitaker House, Kensington, Pennsylvania, 2009, www.whitakerhouse.com

A More Excellent Way to Be in Health, by Henry W. Wright, published by Whitaker House, New Kensington, Pennsylvania, 2009, www.whitakerhouse.com

The Mystery of Spiritual Sensitivity, Your Personal Guide to Responding to Burdens You Feel from God's Heart, by Carol A. Brown, published by Destiny Image Publishers, Inc., Shippensburg, Pennsylvania, 2008, www.destinyimage.com

Jesus, The Greatest Therapist Who Ever Lived, by Mark W. Baker, Ph.D., published by HarperOne, a Division of HarperCollins Publishers, New York, New York, 2007, www.harpercollins.com

The Invisible War, What Every Believer Needs to Know About Satan, Demons, and Spiritual Warfare, by Chip Ingram, published by BakerBooks, a division of Baker Publishing Group, Grand Rapids, Michigan, 2007, www.bakerbooks.com and www.LivingOnTheEdge.org

How to Expel Demons, Break Curses and Release Blessings, by Derek Prince, Ph.D., published by Chosen Books, A Division of Baker Publishing Group, Minneapolis, Minnesota, 2006, www.chosenbooks.com

30 Days to Taming Your Tongue, What You Say (and Don't Say) Will Improve Your Relationships, by Deborah Smith Pegues, published by Harvest House Publishers, Eugene, Oregon, 2005, www.harvesthousepublishers.com

Protecting Your Home from Spiritual Darkness, 10 Steps to Help You Clean House, Place Jesus in Authority and Make Your Home a Safe Place, by Chuck D. Pierce and Rebecca Wagner Sytsema, published by Regal Books, from Gospel Light, Ventura, California, 2004, www.regalbooks.com

Confronting Jezebel, Discerning and Defeating the Spirit of Control, by Steve Sampson, published by Chosen Books, a Division of Baker Book House Co., Grand Rapids, Michigan, 2003, www.bakerbooks.com, and www.SteveSampson.com

The Doubting Disease, Help for Scrupulosity and Religious Compulsions, by Joseph W. Ciarrocchi, published by Integration Books, Paulist Press, New York, 1995

Declaring God's Word, A 365-Day Devotional, by Derek Prince, Ph.D., published by Whitaker House, New Kensington, Pennsylvania, 1995, www.whitakerhouse.com and www.derekprince.org

The Bondage Breaker, Overcoming Negative Thoughts, Irrational Feelings, and Habitual Sins, by Dr. Neil T. Anderson, published by Harvest House Publishers, Eugene Oregon, 1993, Freedom in Christ Ministries, La Habra, California

Released from Bondage, True Stories of Freedom from Obsessive Thoughts, Compulsive Behaviors, Guilt and Hurtful Memories, Satanic Ritual Abuse, Childhood Abuse, and Demonic Strongholds, by Dr. Neil T. Anderson, published by Thomas Nelson Publishers, Inc., Nashville, Tennessee, 1993

The Believer's Authority, by Kenneth E. Hagin, published by Faith Library Publications, Tulsa, Oklahoma, 1986, www.rhema.org

Pulling Down Strongholds, by Derek Prince, Ph.D., published by Whitaker House, New Kensington, Pennsylvania, 1984, www.whitakerhouse.com and www.derekprince.org

The Power of Your Words, If ye shall ask any thing in my name, I will do it, by Don Gossett & E.W. Kenyon, published by Whitaker House, Kensington, Pennsylvania, 1981, www.whitakerhouse.com

Made in the USA
Coppell, TX
10 September 2020

37553510R10048